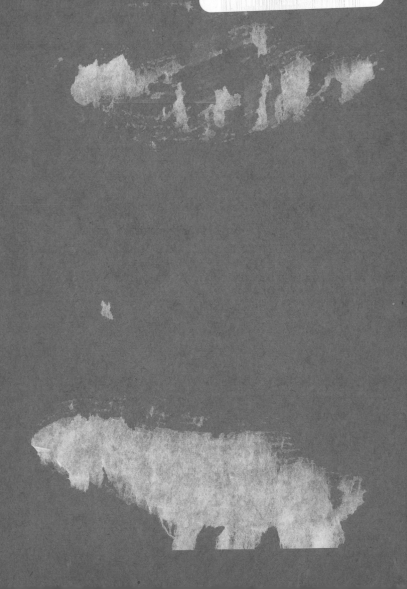

HUNTING
A HAIR SHIRT

AND OTHER SPIRITUAL ADVENTURES

HUNTING
A HAIR SHIRT

AND OTHER SPIRITUAL ADVENTURES

BY

ALINE KILMER

NEW YORK
GEORGE H. DORAN COMPANY

Copyright, 1923,
By George H. Doran Company

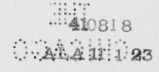
Hunting a Hair Shirt. I

Printed in the United States of America

TO

ÆSCULAPIUS

ACKNOWLEDGMENT

My thanks are due to *The Bookman*, *Harper's Bazar*, *The Lion's Mouth*, *Harper's Magazine*, and *St. Elizabeth's Quarterly*, for permission to reprint several of these pieces.

CONTENTS

ONE: Pernicious Practice of Philosophers

Se moquer de la philosophie c'est vraiment philosophe.

—*Basil Pascal*

ONE: Pernicious Practice of Philosophers

"A HUNDRED years from now," said my nurse rather snappishly, as she combed out my lax drab locks preparatory to winding them on silk strips so that on the morrow I should deceive outsiders into believing that God had given me curly hair, "a hundred years from now, what difference will it make if your hair *was* pulled to-night?"

I protested no more, but knelt meekly before her and submitted to being yanked, not unkindly but most decisively, from side to side. Of course, I might have retorted that in a hundred years it would make no difference whether or not my hair was curled that night. But I was only five and such retorts were beyond me. It seemed to me that her question was unanswerable. Its poison sank deeply into my mind and I have never been the same since.

[13]

I went to bed, and, as I tossed uncomfortably from pillow to post, I assured myself that in a hundred years it would make no difference if the knobs of black silk and silky drab did hurt my head excruciatingly when I lay down. I even went so far as to assure myself that at that remote period it would not matter that my hair had been "dirt-colour" and limp, instead of fluffy and flaxen like my sister's curls. I was hopelessly tainted.

Now, I suppose, in order for my nurse's speech to have had so sinister an effect on my infant mind, the germ of philosophy must already have been there awaiting fertilisation. So my nurse must not be unduly blamed. But this attitude may be recognised as one of the ear-marks. Because she succeeded so fatally well I cannot even blame her for making me into a philosopher. It is an integral part of philosophy to say: "Oh, well, it would probably have happened anyhow." And I do not whole-heartedly regret it. Philosophers never regret anything. They can't. For this reason they never learn anything. It is not for nothing that philosophy is one of the last things taught in our educational institutions. That

[14]

it should be taught at all shows a complete mis-
understanding of the thing.

One of the curious paradoxes of our moral
culture is that we are taught that struggle is
noble: and, almost in the same astonished
breath, we are taught to regard philosophers
with envy and admiration. The envy is un-
derstandable, but why the admiration? The
calm of philosophy is undoubtedly comfortable,
but does it lead anywhere? It is the calm of
death. Who ever heard of a philosopher doing anything? The springs of action are dried
up within him.

Granting the premise that struggle is noble
(though we all spend our infant years in learn-
ing and our years of parenthood in teaching
that it is anything but that); it follows that it
is admirable to do those things that are hardest
for us. Ask any bred-in-the-bone philosopher
whether it is harder for him to struggle or to
endure. Unless the truth is no longer in him,
he will admit that enduring is the easiest thing
he does.

But truth is so seldom in him. This is not
his fault. Truth—surprised, spasmodic truth
—springs so largely from instinct and emotion,

[15]

which things he has crippled to a greater or less degree according to his success in philosophising, that he is incapable of knowing it when he sees it. He will make an effort to side-track you. Truth, he will tell you, is relative. He will gladly and glibly tell you many other things about it, also. You must not expect to escape unscathed. So I think that it will be just as well for you not to ask him. As to whether or not the things he would tell you are true—I cannot be expected to answer that. I have already admitted that I have been a philosopher from the age of five.

TWO: Wicked Wireless

And his servants said to him, Behold,
there is a woman that hath a familiar
spirit at En-dor.
And Saul disguised himself, and put on
other raiment, and he went, and two
men with him, and they came to the
woman by night.

I Samuel 28:7-8

TWO: Wicked Wireless

IT is an evil age in which we live. An evil and a blasphemous age. Ours is the worst form of degeneracy. We take as commonplaces what other ages have held as splendid mysteries or mysterious abominations.

We have profaned the air, we have profaned the sea, and what we have done to the earth is beyond the scope of words. For one instance: what have we done to the Palisades? For miles we have debased them until no one should be able to look upon them without shame. How can they bear with us? One, seeing their abjection, yearns to comfort them —longs to pat the creatures and say, "Never mind, dears. They have brought down your beauty for a time, but to you a thousand years is as a day, and in a thousand years you shall see your petty persecutors blowing like dust across your face. Oak trees shall force them-

selves up through the cities they have builded
and you shall come into your own again." But,
after all, they do not need our pity. Their
pathos is terrible and their patience ominous.
They but bide their time.

And now, surely, we have reached the limits
of enormity. They tell you that for a few
dollars you can wear a little radio on your
wrist! The thing is immodest, indecent, and
immoral. They praise it in the name of
progress!

Profanity is trembling on my lips. Really,
my children, we had those things in Egypt five
thousand years ago. Or, if you are so vulgar
as to ask for proof, at least we had phonographs
and many things that your scientists and inventors would open their eyes to hear described.
By what power did we build the pyramids?
Be modest, I entreat you, until you can answer that. Who is to say that we did not have
wireless?

These things are all right, I grant you, in
their place. But that place is witchcraft. I
have no doubt there was a sending station at
Delphi and that the priestesses at Eleusis wore
little radios in their fillets. But they respected

these tremendous powers. They didn't stifle the imaginations of their clients by giving away the whole show.

I am not denying the real uses of wireless. I should be the last to object to it if it were handled with dignity and beauty. Each ship should number among its crew a magician who would signal for help in case of need. His apparatus and himself should be regarded with awe and veneration. Pomp and circumstance should attend the rare occasions on which he would send out the Macedonian cry—S.O.S. As Stevenson has said, "Any fine action is the better for a little piece of purple." But when John Jones is in the middle of the ocean, John Jones *is* in the middle of the ocean, and it is not for you and not for me to talk to him. Why annihilate time and space impertinently?

As for political communications, they would probably be all the better for a little delay. In many cases international trouble might be avoided by simply sending no messages at all. Most troubles solve themselves if left wisely alone. In extreme cases, rulers could seek wizards, as rulers have done before now.

We are so hopelessly conceited! In our

ravings about what we have achieved, we forget Friar Roger in the thirteenth century. He was a wise and virtuous man. He gave us gunpowder because he knew it would be good for us. Automobiles he withheld, foreseeing that they would increase crime and disease. But he knew as much about automobiles as we do. And besides, he had a Talking Head. Dame Alice Kyteler would smile at our fatuousness in thinking ourselves advanced. What, think you, did she use in assembling her witches and their familiars for a Walpurgis Nacht?

A sharp line should always be drawn between Black Magic and White Magic. If, as the beguiling advertisements claim, any child can operate a radio, does it follow that any child *should* operate a radio? No child of mine has yet, thank God, shown any such abnormal ability, but, should one do so, I should feel it my duty to apprentice him at once to a wise and benevolent magician who would bring him up in the paths of White Magic.

I do not understand wireless. I do not want to understand wireless. I consider it one of those mysteries that should be revealed only to a chosen few. We are doing a rash and dangerous thing in putting such a tremendous power into hands that will make we know not what use of it.

It is in the manner of use that all the difference lies. In other ages, when the devotees of magic have regarded it with reverence and used it with wisdom, they have been called magicians and sorcerers. They have been revered and rewarded: and so they should be. When they have regarded it wickedly and used it wantonly, they have been called witches and warlocks. They have been burned at the stake: and so they should be. It remained for us to show an amazing callosity. We live in a perpetual witches' Sabbath and we don't care at all. As Richard Le Gallienne has said somewhere, we have perverted Emerson's advice until we now feel that the only purpose of the celestial bodies is to draw our wagons.

And with it all, by what jot or tittle have we added to the sum of human happiness? We can, forsooth, listen to lectures when we are not there. Surely there is something obscene in the thought. And who wants to listen to lectures, anyhow? Most people would go far to avoid them. We have ennobled nothing that we have touched. When our vaunted civilisation has been lost in the mists of antiquity and our triumphs have passed into legend, who among our inventors will match with Dædalus, who in a moment of stress constructed practicable wings? Who among our aviators will match with Icarus who flew too near the sun? We shall leave behind us no pyramids and sphinxes to hint at our glories. We but scar the face of nature with our scratching. Two thousand years from now some archæologist may discover the skeleton of a skyscraper, but I am sure he will shake his head over it and consider it pretty poor picking.

THREE: Those Unruly Emotions

O, I got a zoo, I got a menagerie inside
my ribs.

—*Carl Sandburg*

THREE: Those Unruly Emotions

EMOTIONS are much like children. A certain amount of discipline is good and necessary for them. But if you discipline your emotions too severely you are in danger of becoming one of those terrible persons whose emotions come when they are called. By this it is not meant definitely that children should not come when they are called but rather that they should not be always slavishly at hand awaiting a call. Healthy children should sometimes be out of hearing and other sometimes they should be present when they are not at all desired. And again when you call one child another, who happens to be nearer, may answer. And it is the same with emotions. They should not be crushed past the possibility of revolt.

I know a lady—a youngish lady—in whose company I take great delight. The main reason I enjoy her is because she is so unexpected. Perhaps if I knew her better I should like her less. But as it is she piques me pleasantly. She is rather a stern, uncompromising person. You would think she ruled her emotions with a rod of iron. But I went to the circus with her one day and to my horror and embarrassment at the time and my intense amusement later, instead of "registering" enjoyment and interest, or even mild boredom, she wept aloud through the whole thing. She cried with heavy sobs like the mock turtle, and dripped great tears all over the magazine that I gave her to distract her attention from the things that were breaking her heart.

It was a case of the wrong child responding to a call. The emotion that was on top was the one that appeared, and by this I knew that her emotions were very properly alive and that in spite of her usual repression of them they could still act on their own initiative. This, of course, may be considered an ideal example.

While emotions should not be crushed past the possibility of revolt, neither should they have daily exercise like a horse. The man who has displayed his temper so often that it has lost its effect is even more contemptible than the man who has subdued his temper until he cannot lose it when he should.

But we must not neglect the noble army of sentimentalists. There are so many of them that perhaps we should have attended to them first. Think of all the awful people you know with neat sets of emotions as dead as chessmen and with as carefully planned moves. These emotions they move back and forth before you on appropriate occasions, and they never make false plays. In solemn moments they wear long faces, and I know their thoughts are solemn. In sorrowful moments they weep with well-trained eyes into scented handkerchiefs that have never been mislaid.

But they are much more horrible than chessmen, these mechanical emotions. They are a dreadful travesty of life——like children stuffed and worked by electricity. And they have a most stultifying effect on the emotions of others. Any real, live emotion will shut itself up sulkily within a shell when brought into association with these automatic creatures. You cannot even laugh naturally in their presence. And, by the way, people who possess

these horrid automata seldom laugh except at
funny stories. All the exquisite humour of daily
events is lost to them. You never see them going about their ordinary duties laughing in-
sanely and deliciously at the absurd ideas that
will turn up in the best regulated minds. They
are all too unlike the adorable little girl who
didn't mind punishment because when put in
a corner with her face to the wall she could
"fink funny foughts." They have sometimes
a carefully cultivated irrelevance which passes
with them for whimsicality. But above all,
they always take themselves with an absolutely
terrifying seriousness. They consider themselves misunderstood and ill-treated by the
world. They would be regarded as tragic figures. And tragic figures they are—but they
will never know why.

Then there are the people who have a great
many very much alive emotions. They keep
them in cages, so to say, and only let them out
occasionally. They never let them out for me.
But they let them out for Amaryllis. Amaryllis
came in one evening and told me of a lady with
whom she had just dined.

"She had a whole zoo full of emotions and she let 'em all out at dinner," she said.

I expressed sympathy but Amaryllis refused it with scorn. "Oh, no," she said, "I like it. You get so inside of people. Of course you don't always think what they would like for you to think, but you get to know a lot about them."

But it's a dangerous sport, this watching other people's zoos on parade. For usually they soon regret having opened the cage doors. They feel that they have made fools of themselves and they very naturally hate you for it.

All things considered I am glad people don't pour out their souls, or lions and zebras, if you will, to me. It would embarrass me, and as I am no dissembler I probably could not act up to the occasion. Besides, I am too busy. I have a few well-filled cages of my own and it takes all my spare time keeping them fed and watered.

FOUR: Hope

Lasciate ogni speranza voi che'ntrate.
—*Dante Alighieri*

FOUR: Hope

THERE'S no doubt about it," I said to Alpheus. "Hope is a most undesirable thing. We should be infinitely better off without it." Alpheus looked surprised at my vehemence.

"Hope?" he said. "Why hope is merely a physical attribute, like—like red hair. Either you have it or else you haven't, and I can't see that it makes much difference."

I didn't contradict Alpheus. He has a nimble mind and I have not. It is necessary for me to take an idea away and mumble it in private as a dog does a bone. Once, long ago in my impetuous youth, I fell unprepared into an argument and the result was so humiliating that I did not speak again for ten years, except to ask someone to pass me the bread or something like that. This experience has taught me a measure of caution. Also, it has lent me a touch of what I have heard mistakenly called mystery. So I did not contradict Alpheus.

Nevertheless, I think he is all wrong. Hope is much more like tonsillitis than it is like red hair. It is a state—an abnormal state. And having been in it once carries no assurance that we will not be in it again. Hope springs eternal, as we have been told.

I am writing in what Alpheus calls a spirit of fine Christian cynicism. But I realise that the bulwarks of favourable prejudice that have been built up around hope will lead many to suppose that this remark was ironical. I need only refer such to the "Pilgrim's Progress." The Shepherd Boy was an admirable character, and was it not he who sang in the Valley of Humiliation, "He that is down need fear no fall"? There is really nothing un-Christian in my attitude. It does not lead to pessimism. If you should not keep your eyes on the stars and fall into a ditch, neither should you watch your feet and bump your head against the mantelpiece. The middle course is always the sane one.

The hope that in the Scriptures is linked up with faith and charity is an altogether different matter. (Theologians, *à moi!*) We are not bidden to hope that we will be happy or prosperous in this life any more than we are bidden to have faith in the stock market. In fact, we are told over and over again that all flesh is grass, that moth and rust will corrupt, that from him that hath not shall be taken away even that which he hath, and other things of a like desperate character. I am not speaking of the Theological Virtues. So I beg that I be not regarded as heretical.

The Ancients, the Very Ancients, I think understood well that hope was only another trouble in Pandora's box, all the more dangerous because superficially attractive. The light-minded comparative moderns who followed on their heels read their false philosophy into the tale and garbled it—I had almost said hopelessly. Originally, I am convinced, hope was simply the last straw.

The most serious charge I have to bring against hope is that it leads to spiritual degradation and moral degeneration. As I have been unable to lead anyone to dispute this point

[37]

with me, I take it that it is indisputable and dispose of it rapidly. With hope you readily take to low courses that in a proper state of hopelessness you would never contemplate. It has the ruinous properties of some drugs. Without hope, it is comparatively easy to be reckless of consequences in pursuit of the right. Hope, even more than conscience, makes cowards of us all.

A less serious but even more unpleasant result of yielding to hope is the loss of contentment. You may be going happily along your hopeless way, expecting nothing, dreading nothing, being thankful in your humble fashion that the worst has never yet befallen you. Suddenly hope hits you between the eyes. Gone is your peace of mind. Your simple pleasures lose their savour because your heart is fixed on something beyond them. You are content with nothing. Your state is one of feverish anxiety.

And what does it all profit you? If you are balked of what you are hoping for, you are plunged into some degree of despair, which is an even less desirable state than that of hope. Or, granted that you get it—and not being a pessimist I will allow that the chances are at

least even—either you will get it after you have
long ceased to want it, when it is dust and
ashes on your tongue; or you will find, when
you have it, that it does not mean so much to
you as you had thought it would; or, under the
most favourable conditions, you get it, you gloat
over it for a varying length of time. Then, in
the nature of events, it is gone or you are ac-
customed to it and you go foolishly to work
hoping for something else, not realising that
the former hope has spoiled part of your life
for you. For my own part I had far rather
find an adder in my bed than a hope in my
heart.

The piteous part of it all is that you might
have got the thing just as well without hoping
for it. For, of course, I do not advocate the
slackening of effort in the absence of hope.
And, indeed, even better results should be obtained through conservation of the energies that
are constantly being frittered away in hoping.

There is little of the reformer's instinct in
me. If I had more I should probably start a
crusade to abolish hope. As it is, I am doing
something in a modest way. It is my enviable
lot to have several children to bring up. I am

preparing them to meet life in the way that I think will ensure them a minimum of pain. I am bringing them all up without hope.

So far, my success has been astonishing. My eldest child is now quite advanced in years. He is utterly hopeless. The others, though they have imbibed the Shepherd Boy's Song in the Valley of Humiliation with their bottles, and though they seem to have realised from birth the truth of the proverb, "He who sits on the ground cannot fall down," I had considered too young to be judged in this regard. But recently I received a promising indication in the case of my daughter, who is the eldest of this group.

I was rather depressed about her to begin with. Someone had said to me: "What a great deal of love your little girl must have received. I never saw so affectionate and trusting a child!" I quaked inwardly. Was this the fruit of all my efforts? So I took her away for a visit, thinking a change might do her good. And Marjorie appeared.

Marjorie was the child of a neighbour and played constantly with the daughter of my hostess. "Is it possible," I wondered, "for any human being to be as namby-pamby as that child looks?" I decided in the negative. "Probably," I thought, "she is a seething maelstrom of emotions underneath." And I was right.

Florence, the daughter of my hostess, was imperious, brilliant, fascinating. The dullest eye could see that Marjorie adored her. My fragile, harmless child appeared and the elements were unloosed. Marjorie, with no shadow of warning, leapt from the shrubbery beside the house upon my child, beat her, threw her off the veranda and kicked her. Then she fled before vengeance could be wrought. They came to me, Florence chattering with indignation, my daughter calm, examining her wounds speculatively. There was a primitive thrill in their tale that stirred me. I felt like giving loud cheers for Marjorie even while my arm stole round my injured lamb. But this feeling, I knew, was reprehensible, so I merely asked my daughter what she had done to provoke the attack.

"Not anything," she said. "I never saw her before."

A toneless statement of fact has seldom

moved me as this did. I felt as proud of her as I did of her assailant. But it seemed that I must dissemble all my enthusiasms this day.

"Marjorie just jumped right out of the bushes!" Florence repéated. I turned to my child.

"Well, weren't you surprised at that?" I asked with cheerful inanity. But she shook her head.

"No," she said, with a simple resignation that would have moved a stone.

Since then my mind has been at ease about her. She is prepared for life. Now I can devote my energies toward training my younger children. If I achieve such success with them I am sure that my family when it is grown will arise and call me blessed. But if they do not I shall not be pained.

FIVE: A Study in Economy

"It was a miracle of rare device,
A cunning pleasure-dome with caves of ice."
—*Samuel Taylor Coleridge*

FIVE: A Study in Economy

IT had become obvious that the economics
of my household were seriously out of
order. I detached myself with a severe
wrench from things that interested me more
and, in an evil hour, set my mind, for which
I have always had the highest regard, to the
task of discovering the leaks. I hated to do
a thing like this to my mind, but I consoled it
by whispering that the agony would be brief.
I was always an optimist.

In the first place, I soon found that my household accounts were not in such condition that
I could without a qualm hand them over to
an inspector. But, after diving about among
bills and cheque-stubs, I made many discov-
eries. The worst of these was that in no way
could expenses be materially reduced. Except
in the case of the ice-bills. It came upon me

with a shock that my monthly ice-bill was now equal to the amount I had paid for rent in the care-free days before perforce I had become a landed proprietor. This must be stopped at once. I went to the cook.

"Oh, that ice-box!" she wailed. "It simply burns up ice!"

I could well believe it. I examined the thing. The doors were warped almost beyond recognition from living in the open—if the latticed back-porch may be so called. Also there were signs that the bottom was in danger of dropping out. A new ice-box was evidently essential.

"Do nothing in a hurry," I murmured to myself, it having been borne in upon me through long years that I was prone to impulsive action—when I acted at all. So I slept on this.

In the morning, what I then took to be the hand of God brought me the advertisement of a famous firm of refrigerator-builders who were selling throughout that week refrigerators of all sorts and sizes at thirty-three and one-third per cent discount. I should scarcely have dared to disregard so clear a call.

Later in the week I visited the showrooms of these philanthropists. I wish I had died first.

There it stood, in the midst of lesser lights. My blossom, my darling, the apple of my eye! A miracle of pale blue and silver. My heart became as water within me, so great was my desire.

The discount would bring its price, I found, just below two hundred dollars, and by a joyous coincidence I had just two hundred dollars in the bank. I could pay for it and still retain a balance, small indeed, but still a balance. As to the future—well, with that ice-box by my side I could face penury without a quiver.

So I sealed the bargain and they promised to send with it, without charge, a bonnie wee table of gleaming white enamel to keep it company. I wonder sometimes, in dark moments, if they were such keen psychologists as to understand the importance of this act that they appeared to think one of supererogation. Already I was beginning to realise that there was nothing in my home worthy to associate with that ice-box. The piano was the only article I owned that had cost more, and it among

[47]

pianos was not in the same class as that ice-box among ice-boxes.

I went home walking on air. My purse was light, but so was my heart, so what did it matter?

After a few days of agonised waiting, it came, my jewel of jewels, my lily of ice-boxes! As it was being uncrated in the back-yard I watched from a window, my hands over my plunging heart. Inaudibly I sang to myself "The Little Red Lark." Inapplicable? Perhaps, but not altogether so.

> "O swan of slenderness, dove of tenderness,
>   Lily of light, arise!
> But till thou'rt risen earth is a prison
>   Full of my hopeless sighs.
> Awake and discover to thy fond lover
>   The morn of thy matchless eyes."

Then, without warning, the trouble began. It took five men two hours to move the old ice-box from its moorings. It was an honest, cumbrous creature. It cost five dollars to have its remains decently interred. It took the same five men three hours to set the new favourite on the throne of the old. And the whole house creaked and groaned under the strain. I paced the library with my hands over my ears as one awaiting the birth of his first child. Anon I sank at my desk with my head on my arms. What if—what if—Ah, no. It was too dreadful to think of. Nothing could happen to my beloved ice-box. Its glistening surface of tender blue enamel would surely move even those hard hearts and horny hands to unwonted gentleness.

At last its lamentations ceased. I crept forth tremblingly to see how my darling looked in her new setting.

Ah, there she was! A glory in the gloom of the latticed back-porch. The lattice was broken in several places and the floor was scored and scarred unmercifully, but on the ice-box herself only a few scratches on the silver bands told of the awful struggle.

For a month all seemed to be going well. Then one sad morning the cook came to me and told me that the back-porch was sinking.

Now by this time, such is the instability of the human heart, my ice-box no longer thrilled me. I felt somewhat irritated at her for causing me this desperate annoyance. But she was mine, irrevocably chosen by me from among

[49]

all ice-boxes. It was not her fault, but my unparalleled misfortune that she was too heavy for my house. The time for me to consider her disqualifications was past. I have always striven to live up to my responsibilities. It was up to me to provide a suitable home for my ice-box.

It may be thought that the mere sinking of a back-porch is not a thing to cause such distress as I endured over it. The rebuilding or strengthening of a porch may seem a simple affair. But those who know me will understand that with me it was an incurable affliction. With me such things are irremediable.

"A lost thing could I never find,
Nor a broken thing mend."

I knew at once that the only thing for me to do was to buy another house.

So I began my search. Diligently I sought. House after house I rejected because its foundations did not impress me as sturdy enough to support the weight of my ice-box. Finally, after months of seeking, I found a house builded upon a rock. Impulsively I bought it, mortgages and all.

I moved. Alas, too soon I discovered that
a firm foundation was not all I required. There
was so little room in my new house that my
ice-box had not where to lay its head. There
was no back-porch; there was no front porch;
there was no pantry. The kitchen was too
small, the dining-room was too small. The
living-room was on the second floor and so out
of the question. I racked my brain for a solu-
tion, while my ice-box waited for days out of
doors.

At last I was forced to a painful compromise.
By performing a rather serious operation on the
kitchen, standing-room within its shelter could
be provided for the ice-box until such time as
I should have recovered sufficiently to build an
addition. In another year I may have made
enough money to do this. But the thought
overshadows me cruelly. It would be easier for
me to build that addition with my bare hands
than to engage a builder. In fact, unless one
comes knocking at my door, I do not see how it
is to be done at all.

Meanwhile I have reformed. I shall never
economise again. I may see my household go-

[51]

ing to rack and ruin for lack of the timely out-
lay of a little money but I, in my dear-bought
wisdom, shall smile placidly and watch it
go.

SIX: Relativity

My dog is rabid and my cat is lean,
And not a pot in all this house is clean,
The locks have fallen from my hingeless
    doors,
And holes are in my credit and my floors.
                 —*Anna Wickham*

SIX: Relativity

SINCE calling on Evadne to-day I have been in an even more self-satisfied state than usual.

I can scarcely say that Evadne is a friend of mine. No one knows enough about her, in spite of her beautiful frankness, to be justified in making so rash a statement. But at least I can say that I am a friend of Evadne's. And it is difficult to see why anyone should want me as a friend. I have few convictions, and those I have I won't talk about; my sympathies are well under control (this is not due to hardness of heart but to my Cubist point of view), and my personality is so negligible that I never made a remark in general company in my life without being interrupted. This, of course, is why I am driven to express myself in writing.

But this is enough of me. I was, for some

[55]

reason or other, wishing that God had made me a practical woman. It seemed to me eminently desirable that I should be one. This train of thought becoming painful, I went for a walk and met Evadne. She is short and plump and pretty and looks no more than her age.

First having been assured that her husband was not at home—he is one of those tall, straight, bending-from-the-hips Englishmen, with perfectly immobile faces—I returned with her.

A log fire was burning in her living-room as we entered and the maid (Evadne's maids are always like undesirable members of the family) was watching it anxiously. It was a strange fire. The thick end of a dead branch about six feet long was burning furiously on the hearth, and the other end protruded toward the middle of the room.

"I couldn't help it," said the maid with friendly apology. "But there wasn't no more wood and the axe was up in your bedroom."

"In my bedroom!" gasped Evadne faintly, but the girl had flown.

Evadne cast me a look of amused dismay. I was frankly convulsed. We sat down to tend the fire, feeding the branch in carefully until we could thrust one end up the chimney. The children could be heard raging upstairs, but Evadne's face remained calm.

"I've been wishing that I were a practical woman," I said, merely to start her.

She faced me with astonishment.

"Good Lord, why?"

I tried to fix myself firmly at one of my many angles of vision.

"Everything would be so much simpler, and I should be a much nicer person."

"You must be mad!" All her statements are emphatic.

But here, somewhere in the upper regions, a child fell downstairs with great effect. Evadne evidently recognised the shrieks. She merely went to the foot of the stairs and listened a moment. Then she returned to her seat by the fire and repeated her remark even more firmly.

"You must be mad. Nothing could be further from the truth than those two statements. Everything is much more complex for practical persons, and as for you"—she made a gesture as of one snuffing a candle—"you'd simply be gone."

I shrank back into my deep chair in humiliation, and she dashed on.

"Take me, now. Do you call me a practical person?" I grinned. "I do not."

She was openly triumphant.

"Well, what do I do? I satisfy a man whom most women would find it difficult to satisfy, I manage a large house, and while I should hesitate to say that I manage the children, at any rate I keep them alive. And when you consider that there are six of them and at least one of them is always ready to do murder, that is something to be able to boast. If I were a practical woman I should by this time be either a lunatic or a drudge, while as it is——"

"While as it is you are unbearably conceited," I finished for her. She smiled complacently.

"Be that as it may. But I am very happy, and so are all the rest of the family." A series of horrible shrieks gave the lie to this statement. We dashed upstairs, Evadne gurgling with laughter.

"It's only Nicholas," she called to me over her shoulder. "He's not hurt. He just has a vile temper, you know."

[58]

Nicholas and Rosamond were pulling at opposite ends of a dilapidated woolly lamb. The lamb came in two as we entered the nursery, and they both sat down violently with redoubled howls. A Belgian hare slept tranquilly on the hearth; a tiny fairy-like creature of two played with a monkey-wrench on the floor near a bassinet where the baby sat watching the scene wide-eyed. "Mommie," she gurgled joyously when she saw us, deftly dropping the monkey-wrench in on the baby.

"It's my belief that you're all mad except the baby," I said as we returned to the fire, "and he's too young to be judged."

"Oh, no, he isn't," Evadne replied earnestly. "You can tell almost at once." She would undoubtedly have plunged into her theories about judging the sanity of babies from birth, but at this instant tea and her sister arrived simultaneously.

From the moment her sister entered there was a change in Evadne. She seemed worried. She poured the tea clumsily. She leapt nervously at every sound from above. She left long, awkward gaps in the conversation unfilled. But the conversation had really ceased to be conversation, anyway. Things were very stupid all through tea.

Evadne's sister is older than Evadne. She is a monstrously capable person. Also she was gazing coldly around the large, comfortable, pleasant but disorderly room, and looking inquiringly at the baby whom Evadne had brought down and who was crawling about the floor, looking like a live mop.

"Evadne," she asked sternly, "did my furs ever come?"

Evadne shook her head mournfully. Her sister turned to me and explained.

"I ordered my furs sent here from the cleaner's because we were all away and the cleaner was going to move. I don't understand it at all. I gave them the full address—20 Hillside Avenue. I saw the man write it down. Do you suppose they *can* have gone anywhere else?" This to Evadne.

"There's another family of the same name here," Evadne said listlessly. All spirit seemed to have gone out of her. She looked physically smaller.

"I'll call them up and find out," her sister

[60]

said firmly. "But they had the *Street number*. I don't see how they could have gone wrong."

"Maybe they didn't see the number," I suggested idiotically. "Or it may be worn off."

"Perhaps. But street numbers should be prominent. Where *is* the number on your house, Evadne?"

Terror leaped into Evadne's eyes.

"I don't know," she murmured feebly. Her sister stared at her aghast.

"Don't know where your own street number is? I never heard of such a thing in my life!" Evadne waved a despairing hand.

"But, Hester, I should think I'm the one person who doesn't need to know where this house number is. I'm *inside* the house. And when I'm outside I know where the house is, and that's better than knowing where the number is."

But Hester was not to be so easily beguiled. She fixed Evadne with an eye that forbade flippancy.

"How do the tradespeople find your house number?" she asked severely. Evadne made a dying effort. She stirred with something like irritation.

[61]

"Oh, they know how to find such things. They're trained observers."

I could bear no more, so I slipped away. As I stood outside the door bidding farewell to them I whispered to Evadne:

"The number is on the left hand side of the door frame." She smiled her thanks and I left her to her fate.

But I had obtained more comfort than I had hoped for. Evadne was by far the more enjoyable creature of the two. There was much in what she said about the drawbacks of practicality. But perhaps the main reason that I am comforted is that beside Evadne I feel practical and efficient. There is no one else who gives me this sensation. I shall call on Evadne again soon, and I hope that this time her sister will not come.

SEVEN: Hunting a Hair Shirt

"I clearly see, some one will say, of what profit, and how necessary mortification is, however I cannot at the same time but think of the pain and difficulty found therein; and it is *this* which deters me from it."

—*V. F. Alphonsus Rodriguez*

SEVEN: Hunting a Hair Shirt

LET it be distinctly understood that I do not want a hair shirt. I have no idea that I ever shall want one. But if I should—I say impressively—if I ever should want one, I think the getting of it should be a simpler matter than it is. As the White Knight said of the mouse-trap that he carried on his saddle, you never know when you may need a thing. Think of it! Suppose, in some perfectly unforeseen moment, it was brought home to you that a hair shirt you must have. How on earth would you get it? You would not care to invest in a hair shirt simply because some day the spirit of penitence might seize you. But if, on the other hand, that day should arrive, it would be embarrassing to be forced to ask everyone you met where such a garment might be obtained.

For a long time I pondered the subject deeply.

I would not ask anyone. I was too proud. I
supposed everyone else knew and that I was in
a lonely depth of ignorance. So I was very
stealthy about it. I sought secretly and eagerly
for signs or advertisements that might read
"Spring Novelties in Hair Shirtings" or "Cus-
tom-Made Hair Shirts," so that at least I might
learn whether you bought them by the yard or
had them tailored for you. It even occurred
to me that they might be found ready-to-wear
in a department store. I pictured myself ap-
proaching a haughty saleslady and asking her
timidly if she could direct me to the section
where they sell hair shirts. I am brave and
I might have brought myself to do this, if I
had really wanted that shirt. But, you see, I
didn't. And the signs failed me. I never saw
a sign that even remotely hinted at hair shirts.

I became discouraged. Life is so unneces-
sarily complicated and outrageously artificial.
If I had wanted a piece of wood painted to
represent a basket of flowers and weighted for
its homely duty of holding the door open, I
should have had no trouble. I could easily have
found rubbers for dogs and elaborately uphol-
stered bassinets for cats who prefer to sleep in

the cellar by the furnace. But a simple, medi-
iæval garment like a hair shirt seemed to be out
of reach.

"Can it be," I thought despairingly, "that the
demand for them has decreased so that there is
no longer any incentive to anyone to make
them?" But in happier moments I was more
sane and put thoughts like that determinedly
from me. Penitence must be as sincere as ever,
though it may be less general in its severity.
The rarity of its severe forms should not stop
the manufacture of hair shirts. Carters, I know
it to my sorrow, are extremely rare, yet smocks
blossom on every hand.

So I decided that more direct methods must
be tried. But my spirit quailed at the thought
of asking people. It happens that I have had
to ask for so much useful information in my
life that I am ashamed to do it. I never know
where to go to pay taxes or to vote. I don't
know the difference between the North River
and the Hudson—and that I shall never have
the courage to ask. Even simple things like
getting a carpenter to mend the lattice under
the porch where the children went through after
the rabbit are utterly beyond me.

Keeping in mind this failing of mine and the reputation I am fast acquiring of being an idiot, I hoped I might manage it by indirect discourse, so to say. I would be very wily, tactfully lead the conversation in the desired direction and watch the result.

I found it unexpectedly difficult to steer conversation in the direction of hair shirts without using force. You have no idea how hard that is unless you have tried it. But I waited, hungrily watching for an opening. At last it came.

It was at dinner at the house of Amaryllis. Amaryllis lives next door to me. This evening she seemed somewhat distrait. I enquired the reason of this, as she usually keeps up the dinner conversation with a hectic eagerness that speaks volumes for her early training.

"It's my Belgian andirons," she said readily. "I can't get anyone to make tails for them. That is," for Amaryllis is very conscientious, "they weren't exactly Belgian andirons. The Belgian refugee who sold them to me said she had bought them in Newark. That is—she wasn't really a Belgian refugee. Her husband was——"

"But you say they are hard to get?" I demanded, switching her back to the main point. Amaryllis is discursive.

Amaryllis said they were. It appeared that she had been looking for a blacksmith to complete the almost-Belgian andirons bought from the almost-Belgian refugee. "But blacksmiths are almost extinct since motors came in," she ended sadly. I took no heed of her sorrow. My chance had come.

"So many things are hard to get," I broke in feverishly. "Now, hair shirts, for instance."

I said it with great earnestness, but everybody seemed to think that I had made a joke. They laughed in a way that would have delighted me if I really had made one. But no one volunteered a suggestion, and I realized that that way wouldn't work.

So, a few days later, I gathered myself together and asked Amaryllis in private. Amaryllis is the sort of person you do ask. In the first place she knows almost everything. In the second and more important place she never jeers at you for your ignorance, nor even seems surprised that you don't know.

"Amaryllis," I said, somewhat timidly, "if

[69]

you wanted a hair shirt, where would you go to get it?"

"I'd buy an old sofa and cut it down," said Amaryllis just like that. And she would, too. But this seemed to me extreme.

"You know I can't sew," I said crossly, "and besides, I couldn't afford it." But Amaryllis was now hot on the trail.

"I never really thought about it before," she said with deep and, to me, gratifying interest. "There should be hair shirt emporiums or factories or something. We'll ask everyone until we find out."

I consented, as there seemed no other way for me to get one in case of need, unless I sat up nights and wove my own hair, that being the only hair available. There was, I remembered, an old lady in a fairy tale who wove her own hair into cloth. It always grew again by morning. Mine wouldn't, so I did not like this idea. Also, I had no loom.

As time went on our quest assumed almost national proportions. I went travelling and asked people in all walks of life, but received no sensible replies. Then at home the table talk usually drifted automatically into a discussion of ways and means. Sometimes I almost wished I had not started it.

"They are woven in convents," once mused some gentle and dreamy soul, "of the hair of the nuns, which is cut four times a year."

The thought of the nuns I knew engaged in weaving shirts of hair made me giggle.

"Nonsense!" I exclaimed wildly. "The best ones are made of horse hair."

"They are made of camel's hair," said the beardless cousin of Amaryllis with an air of omniscience. Amaryllis upheld me stoutly.

"They aren't. I know they're made of horse hair. Don't you remember?

'And a shirt of the roughest and coarsest hair
For a year and a day, Sir Ingoldsby, wear.'

That proves it. Horse hair *is* the roughest and coarsest." Amaryllis proves most things by the Ingoldsby Legends. "But they must be woven on hand looms," she went on thoughtfully.

"Hairlooms," said some flippant person in the background.

But light came at last. Father Agrippa came to dinner at my house. I had not seen him for

[71]

a long time. He *does* know everything. So I asked him. He beamed.

"You get them from the monasteries of the penitential orders, of course. Franciscans, for instance. Where you get the chains, you know."

"The chains!" we exclaimed in chorus, aghast.

"Yes. The chains with the points turned in that you wear on your arm or waist. I'll be glad to send you one. The simplest thing in the world. But it would never do for it to be opened in the post office. It must be marked 'Private'—yes, 'Private and Penitential' would be better." He smiled happily.

"But, Father Agrippa," I said meekly, but with desperate firmness, "I don't want"—— He contemplated me rather sadly.

"No," he admitted. "No, I don't suppose you do. And I'm afraid it wouldn't do you any good, anyhow. But"—— he brightened up and turned around hopefully "I shall send one to Amaryllis tomorrow."

EIGHT: Ghoulies and Ghaisties

From ghoulies and ghaisties,
Long leggity baisties,
    And things that go bump in the night:
    Good Lord, deliver us.
                        —*Old Litany*

EIGHT: Ghoulies and Ghaisties

"From ghoulies and ghaisties,
   Long-legged baisties,
   And things that go bump in the night:
   Good Lord, deliver us."

SOMETHING went bump in the night last night. It must have been somewhere on the wrong side of midnight. It was a sharp rap, full of meaning. Alert at once, I stiffened under the bedclothes, not even daring to indulge the impulse to bury my head under the pillows. So tense that I quivered, I lay listening for the sound to be repeated so that I might place it. There was absolutely no sound in all the wide, black world. For what seemed æons of anguished waiting I lay.

Then, horrors! What was that? A tiny pattering, so faint that it seemed rather to be felt than heard, approached from somewhere out

[75]

in the void. Long-leggity baisties tiptoeing daintily across the lawn and peering with evil eyes into my window, the long legs supplemented by even longer necks, flashed across my brain. I could almost have sworn they flashed across my vision. But it was only that inner eye that Wordsworth so misguidedly called "the bliss of solitude." Desperately I tried to move. But it was too late. Fear held me motionless.

In this fearful condition, lying on my back, with aching eyes striving in vain to pierce the surrounding blackness, I experienced a sensation to which I was not altogether a stranger. My ears seemed to grow out until they extended for about a foot on either side of my head and to take on a separate life of their own. Eagerly they waved themselves about like tentacles sucking in the faint patterings, now drawing nearer and nearer. If I had not been consumed by terror I could have laughed aloud at the grotesque feeling. Suddenly, with a sort of sigh of relief, the creatures contracted themselves to their usual inconspicuous position, lying neatly against my head. They had left the field to me.

But it seemed a full minute before my brain grasped the fact that my ears had relaxed because the pattering footsteps had resolved themselves into a gentle and steady rain. It was my turn to sigh with relief.

All sense of direction had left me long since, but I simply must make a light and get some sense of the commonplaceness of my surroundings. Now was the moment or never at all. Somewhere to my right, I knew, stood my reading lamp on its little table. Cautiously I eased myself over on my right side. I could not reach it. The bed had surely grown wider. It was necessary for me to sit up and, leaning far over, to grope about in the dark, dreading that my hand, sensitised beyond all normality, would touch some awful unfamiliar object. But it didn't. By the grace of God, it didn't! It struck the table and, in course of time, the lamp. I gathered myself together for the shock and snapped on the light.

Cringing from what it might reveal, I probed the furthest corners of the room. Everything was as I had left it when I put out the light. The watch on the table beside the bed said half-past one.

[77]

Relieved beyond expression, I piled up my pillows. I settled myself comfortably and reached for a book. Unsuspectingly I opened it and dived in, forgetting for the moment the forces that were arrayed against me this night. Heavens! It was Algernon Blackwood's "The Empty House." Scowling with fear and hatred, I closed it and laid it aside. This action was inadequate. My gentleness was altogether at variance with my feelings. The truth is that I should have flung that book to the ends of the room—of the earth, had that been possible—if I had dared. It was no book for me in the middle of the night.

Frantically I reached for something more soothing to my leaping nerves. "Love Laughs Last" came back in my delighted hand. I was letting myself down gratefully into its amusing sanity when, with a loud click that hurled me back into chaos, the door three feet from my bedside sprung open. Fascinated with fear, my eyes now behaving somewhat as my ears had previously done, I watched it.

It must now be time for the ghoulies and ghaisties. If it should prove to be only a burglar, how I should welcome him! But that

[78]

door led through my bathroom into the back hall, and from the back hall the stairs went gloomily up to the third floor—the third floor where, according to my West Indian maid, "de ghos's originate." I shuddered. "Oh, Lord," I breathed, "let it be only a ghost that I can see and perhaps I shall not go mad." But nothing came. I could feel the hair slowly blanching on my head.

Gone was all hope of reading. I could not even close the book. I could only lie and suffer. My watch now said three o'clock. If the watch had been on the other side, I could not have seen it. How long, O Lord? I lay and indeed I suffered. The only alleviating thought that came to me through that ghastly night was: "What if the door had opened before I turned on the light?" Then surely I had been a gibbering maniac by now.

Finally when it was plain that something must snap to relieve the hideous strain, there came a sound, a sound that often before I had heard, but never welcomed. Some cats, some heaven-inspired cats, were fighting under my window. Perhaps my own dear James was among them. But whoever you were, O blessed cats, I could have taken you collectively to my bosom. The songs of angels could not have been sweeter. Restored to sanity, I leapt from my bed. With a firm and somewhat indignant hand I closed the door, the dreadful door, but I did not look on the other side of it. That latch, I reflected, was never all that it should be. My watch said half-past four. I snapped out the light and crept wearily into bed. A little wind of morning came through the trees and ruffled the curtains at my windows. It also shook an immature apple from the tree just on my boundary line and the apple fell upon the tin roof of my neighbour's garage with a sharp rap, full of meaning. I smiled. The cats sang on.

> "Music that gentlier on the spirit lies
> Than tired eyelids upon tired eyes!"

I murmured. And I nestled my head into my pillow and slept.

NINE: The Helplessness of Adults

The Child is father of the Man.
—*William Wordsworth*

NINE: The Helplessness of Adults

WHO was the happy idiot who first conceived it—that wide-spread fallacy that teaches us that children are helpless? Probably someone whose offspring had driven him into imbecility (blest man!) and who found, in this blissful state, that the slings and arrows of outrageous children could touch him not and trouble not again.

The truth of the matter is, of course, that children are not helpless at all. We are. We are so completely helpless that in many cases we can only wonder at the magnanimity of children in allowing us to live at all. When their advantage is so great, what but magnanimity prevents their pressing it to the extent of their enormous power? Indeed, children are not given credit for their generous impulses.

Still, this does not strike me as one of those wrongs that cry aloud to be adjusted. The balance is already so heavily in their favour that they can afford to wait for redress until greater evils have been remedied.

This is the nefarious method employed by children. In some underhand way, yet to be accounted for, they get a firm grip on our affections. We never notice what is happening until it is too late. Then they go recklessly ahead. Their tyranny is awful. Sometimes, besotted creatures that we are, we like it. When your young son stands swaying on the very edge of the top step and says, in his imperious way, "Now, you may carry me downstairs," you are pleased to the core. But when he wakes at midnight and screams for the grey flannel elephant that he left in the sand-pile, are you pleased? You get it. Undoubtedly you get it. If you say that you do not there is no one so credulous as to believe you. You go in trailing bath-robe and flapping Japanese slippers and doggishly fetch that elephant—in your teeth, as it were. Is it for love of your young son that you do this? It is not. It is because, if you should not get it, he would continue to

make night hideous and there would be no
sleep for you. And, what is worse, the neigh-
bours would be disturbed. But what would he
care for that? What are the broken slumbers
of the whole world to him?

I speak who know. I am not an outsider or
casual observer of children. I happen to have
children of my own—according to the standard
of the times, many children—and to have been
thrown, perforce, into more or less close con-
tact with them. And I have discovered that
their only weakness, and consequently the sole
hope of the world, lies in the fact that, like the
down-trodden middle-class (with which, in the
words of Clarence Day, "I proudly and rev-
erently take my stand") they know nothing
of the value of concerted action. They are
totally unorganised. This is the great work
that the future holds for us—to prevent the or-
ganization of children. I am not, I think,
strikingly weak-minded, nor are my children
abnormally powerful. But I know well that
if they should mutiny all at once I should be
obliged to walk the plank. With this con-
tingency in mind, I shall, in accordance with
the best tradition of mystery stories, place a

copy of this paper in the hands of my lawyer, or the friend in whom I have most confidence. In case of my sudden disappearance it is to be opened and the world can know approximately what has become of me. But it will be too late then to help me.

To take up the argument. A child is help-less in inverse ratio to his age. He is at the zenith of his powers while he is an infant in arms. What on earth is more powerful than a very young baby? "Babies," said a small boy of my acquaintance, gazing reflectively at a new and screaming infant of my own, "babies," he said, "are the worst race in the world." Now he has a little brother and he does not say such things aloud. It is sometimes dangerous to put an unpleasant truth into words. It gives it substance. And it was a truth that he stated, for babies are the worst race (shall we say?) in the world. They are the worst in that they are the most irresponsible. And irresponsibility is always a menace. As they become older they grow less and less powerful. They assume re-sponsibilities until finally they are completely enmeshed and absolutely helpless. In fact, they are adults. It is true that in rare cases this

[86]

does not happen. There are people of whom you remark sadly, or perhaps a trifle wistfully, "as irresponsible as a baby!" And you have always an underlying fear of such people. A perfectly just and reasonable fear. But, of course, it is only a figure of speech. No adult is really quite so irresponsible as a baby.

The extent to which children control our destinies is dreadful to think upon. They can decide our entire manner of life. You may recollect how, when you tried apartment-house life with your young family, including a baby who burned the midnight oil, you were driven from pillar to post by public opinion. Anonymous letters even were brought to bear. Also there was the ever-present danger of windows. Of course, windows can be barred, but a clever child can always manage to get his head, or other valuable parts of his anatomy, wedged between the bars. Finally, in despair, you moved to the country. But life was not much simpler there. You could, without too much misgiving, allow your baby to live in spite of his habits, but other complications arose. Your young daughter, radiant with the joy of life, sought expression of this joy in a casual moment by lifting herself buoyantly over the stair-rail in the upper hall and falling with a dull thud into the hall below. You poured out a *liqueur*-glassful of brandy to revive her, but she was unable to drink it. While you sat on the floor and keened, with her unconscious form clasped to your bosom, your even younger son drank the brandy and in the ensuing fit of drunkenness wrenched a button from his garments and thrust it up his microscopic nose. When the excitement had died down you waited, limp and dejected, for the verdict of the X-ray. You were completely exhausted by the emotional strain. For by this time such slaves are we that the final evil for us is that anything should befall them.

If children knew, oh, if they only knew their power! It is something absolutely glorious in its immensity. But they do not even see it dimly until it is gone forever. Sometimes, it is true, to the child who is growing a little older, a little less irresponsible, a little more articulate, comes a fleeting glimpse of the splendour that is slipping away from him. (When I say "a little more articulate" I do not wish to be interpreted as pitying the child

who is too young to express himself in words.
Far from it. He does not need speech in order
to get everything he wants, and what can man
do more?) But, indeed, as shades of the prison-
house begin to darken, swift gleams of the de-
parting glory flash across. When my four-year-
old daughter explained to me that she tore up
and ate one of my best-loved books because she
was playing that she was the baby and "the
baby doesn't care what he tears up and eats," I
was, in spite of my baffled fury, smitten with a
sentimental sorrow for her. I felt like ex-
claiming "Ichabod!" In fact, I did say "Ichabod!" rather sheepishly. But she only laughed.
It had not quite departed.

When I had reached this point in writing
down the burning thoughts that sear my brain
whenever I hear people make such idiotic re-
marks as: "How can anyone be harsh to
them? Poor little helpless things!" I thought
with pride that I would show it to Evadne.
She, of all my friends, would realise the great
truth of it. She is a little older than I and has
even more children.

Evadne read it. But when she had read it
she did not look pleased. She lifted a white,

stricken face to mine. "Great Heavens!" she gasped, or words to that effect, for Evadne has been a mother so long that she has learned to use strong language. "Great Heavens! You have destroyed the work of centuries. Do you suppose it was for nothing that that belief was started? Do you, in your conceit, imagine that you are the only one who knows it is a fallacy? Why, the children themselves are the only ones it has ever deceived. And now, you fool, you utter fool, you've told them!"

TEN: The Case of Bluebeard

Yet this alone out of my life I kept
Unto myself, lest any know me quite;
And you did so profane me when you crept
Unto the threshold of this room——
                              —*Edna St. Vincent Millay*

TEN: The Case of Bluebeard

IF Bluebeard had only married Sister Anne she would never have gone snooping around among his secrets. Not since I reached the age of reason have I sympathised with Bluebeard's wife. She was put on her honour and she didn't have any. Of course her name was against her. Maeterlinck tried to make out a case for her, but as it was clearly impossible to defend a lady named Fatima, he called her Ariane. But a lady named Ariane would do the same things as a lady named Fatima, only she would deceive herself into believing that she did them from the noblest motives. A most unpleasant person! Fatimas are really more endurable because they never analyse their motives at all.

Now, Anne was a different character entirely. Only her affection for Fatima—who had always been the black sheep of the family—led her to assist her in her difficulty, and it must have been with much the same feeling that the Brothers slew Bluebeard and saved Fatima. "You don't deserve this protection," we can feel them thinking, "but the family must stand together." A very clannish family they were. Clannishness has its admirable points, but in this case it has always irritated me. I have thought that the Brothers might well have done a clean job by finishing up both Bluebeard and Fatima. I hold no brief for Bluebeard, but certainly, if we have been given all the evidence, Fatima had, so far as she knew, no cause for complaint. She was a monster of ingratitude.

As for Bluebeard himself, while I cannot uphold his behaviour he has my sympathy. He was a well-meaning enough gentleman to begin with, with an abnormally strong sense of honour. This sense of honour was his undoing. It was outraged by his first wife—we are not told what she discovered, but it was probably some quite innocent secret. After this tragedy the poor gentleman became a monomaniac. He was always looking for a lady with a sense of honour. Why could he not have married Sister Anne? How different the story would have been! But the Bluebeards are never attracted by the Sister Annes. They always "fall for" women named Fatima or something equally pernicious, and go through life bearing a grudge against all women in consequence.

With the exception of this important truth the whole story is psychologically bad, and probably the reason for this is that it is not a fairy-story at all. It should be cast out of the society of fairy-stories. Fairy-tales are fundamentally right, and this story is wrong from beginning to end. It is not folk-lore but yellow-journalism. The ugly story of the famous or infamous French Count was taken in comparatively modern times and poured into the mould of a fairy-tale. But it never really fitted the mould. Only to the most superficial is there any resemblance between Fatima and the genuine heroine of folk-lore.

Fairy-tale heroes and heroines are not necessarily creatures possessing all the virtues. Indeed, it is rarely that we find one who has not a redeeming vice. Often they are incurably lazy, sometimes their pride is inordinate, heedless and absent-minded they are almost invariably. And occasionally you find one who is bad-tempered or given to drink. In fact, they are a very weak lot. But we like them the better for their frailties. Does anyone like Fatima the better for hers?

Now, in fairy-tales sins are divided to a certain extent according to sex. It may be due to the chivalrous attitude of the transcriber or it may be a fact that women steal less frequently than men. In a fairy-story a man may steal and steal and be a hero. Women are seldom or never found stealing; but, on the other hand, women are credited with a greater fondness for playing with fire. This is such a delectable failing that it is hard to condemn it. It makes one proud to be a woman to see how, when the lovely young girl sticks her finger into the shaft of golden light, she does it purely from an over-developed sporting instinct, while the king's third and favourite son puts the forbidden golden saddle on the horse merely from cupidity, entirely ignoring the excellent advice that has been given him beforehand, usually by a fox. But dearly, dearly they both pay for their crimes.

It may be argued that Fatima was merely playing with fire. She was not. She was going through her husband's pockets—a miserable, low, contemptible trick. But even if we consent to view it as playing with fire, in a real fairy-tale far from being held up to us as a wronged and innocent woman gloriously righted by the abrupt death of her husband, she would have been obliged to wear out about seven pairs of iron shoes as a penance for that little game.

This is the heart of the difficulty. It is not because she sinned that Fatima is no true heroine. It is because she is never cleansed of her guilt. She never has a pang of remorse, but goes cheerfully along her self-righteous way, expecting and doubtless receiving admiring sympathy from all beholders. She is enviably free from any consciousness of sin. In fairy-tales, as in life, the just man may sin seven times a day, but it is essential that there be sackcloth and ashes somewhere in the offing.

It is very sad that Mr. Thackeray is dead. How well he might have remodelled the story of Bluebeard, as he did other tales, if he had only thought of it. It is pleasant to dream of how he would have done it. Fatima might have been killed, presumably by the Brothers, of course accidentally. Bluebeard, recognising the folly of his first choice would, after a suitable interval, marry Sister Anne and spend his life in a laudable effort to atone for his wild oats. They would have numerous offspring and rear them in the strictest honour and integrity, always holding up before their awed young eyes the terrible picture of what had happened to Aunt Fatima.

ELEVEN: On Works of Reference

Books which are no books.
—*Charles Lamb*

ELEVEN: On Works of Reference

LALAGE, who lives with me, is occasionally moved to bitter lamentations. Anyone who lived with me would lament bitterly on occasion. As a philosopher I can realise this without undue heartburning. But I claim that Lalage is unreasonable in doing this, because she does not lament those things that are really lamentable.

Her chief cause of complaint is that my library contains no works of reference. In vain I tell her that I have a dictionary, the finest of all dictionaries. She only asks me coldly to produce it, and I—I cannot. And she will not accept my unsupported word. I am unable to produce the evidence because of all my books that dictionary is the most butterfly-like. It settles now here, now there, and remains so short a time in each place that Lalage, who has lived with me for eight months, claims with apparent sincerity that she has never seen it. When I have seen it myself I cannot say that I have paid much attention to it, except to experience a pleasantly possessive thrill. I never consult it. I never need to. Usually I can grasp the meaning of an unfamiliar word by the context, and as for spelling—well, I am a good speller. On those rare occasions when I really need to look up a word, my dictionary being so much the will-o'-the-wisp, I have a better and more informative way of looking it up. I take some book that I feel sure will somewhere or other contain the word, and I read through it until my search is rewarded. In this way I refresh my memory of books that I have read, and even sometimes read books that otherwise I never should have read.

Recently I have been informed that this practice of mine is one of the many admirable methods of the Chinese. To find the proper use of a word they search the classics. If that word does not appear in the classics, so much the worse for the word. It dies.

From the actual use I have made of my dictionary I have got little but sorrow. Many

[102]

excellent words are ruined by too definite a knowledge of their meaning. There is the tragic case of "hectic." I had always considered it a highly expressive word. I had used it joyously for years to mean a convenient combination of "nervous," "excitable," "feverish." One ill-starred day I looked it up and I have never been able to use it since. Its actual meaning is so far removed from its meaning as used by me and the vulgar generally that I cannot even remember what it was. No one could be expected to remember it. It simply has nothing to do with the case.

But it is not only a dictionary that Lalage would have me possess. She thinks I should have an encyclopædia. Now this is really the height of folly. She knows that I have not sufficient room for those books that I already own. An encyclopædia is ugly and cumbersome. Also it is an expensive thing.

And to an encyclopædia there is the same serious objection that applies to most works of reference. It is too practical and too detailed. What information the average human mind might conceivably be able to grasp is smothered under a mass of technicalities and so lost.

[103]

I have, for instance, read the article on navigation in an encyclopædia. It was, doubtless, sound and, as such articles go, well constructed. Far be it from me to offer any impertinent, half baked criticism upon it. But the fact remains that not one shred of it clung in my mind. What knowledge I have of seamanship, and it is ample for my needs, I got from "The Hunting of the Snark." From a work like that you learn indelibly. You learn with the Bellman. In company with that intelligent but untrained gentleman, I never knew whether an east wind blew from the east or to the east. It is not a thing one can easily inquire about. One might safely guess at it if it were not for the technical terms. The phrase "due east" is certainly confusing if not deliberately misleading. But after one reading of "The Hunting of the Snark" the truth is fixed in your mind.

I do not think I am peculiar in this. Is there anyone who has not learned more history from historical romances than from the pages of histories themselves? I believe not.

It might be possible, with a little research, to draw up a list of such substitutes to fill the places of all dull reference books on library shelves. Dozens of delectable ones flash into my mind. But I hold my hand because, if I presented this list, I should then be in the despicable position of having perpetrated a work of reference. This I have vowed I shall never do.

So I claim that Lalage is unreasonable. But I think privately that it is better so. Unreason never annoys me. I have with it unfailing patience. If Lalage came to me and complained that my housekeeping compared unfavourably with that of Mrs. Jellyby—if in these benighted days there are many who do not recognise Mrs. Jellyby I am glad of that, because they won't know what I mean—if she pointed out that I begin a thousand things that I never finish, if she showed me that, though I am potentially a capable person, I never accomplish anything, she would be perfectly right. Reason would be all on her side. But then I should be very angry.